The Bible Beautiful Series

The Oldest Bedtime Story Ever

Written and illustrated
by Benjamin Morse

This story goes back to the beginning of time.

It is about the people of Israel

and the God who loved them

and who loves you too.

LIGHT

LET

BE

THERE

Jews first called this collection of ancient writings the Torah.

It was the first Bible.

Christians later named their version of it the Old Testament.

And Muslims included parts of it in their holy book, the Qu'ran.

The Bible uses many titles to describe God:

In those days, no one was supposed to say God's actual name out loud

It is spelled with the Hebrew letters for Y-H-W-H

and read from right to left:

This sacred name comes from the word "to be".

Because God is invisible, the first letter of His name ("yod")

 will appear at important moments

throughout the story

as a sign of His unseen presence.

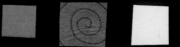

In the beginning,

when God was creating

the heavens and the earth

from the wild

and formless darkness,

God's voice rushed over the

deep waters and said,

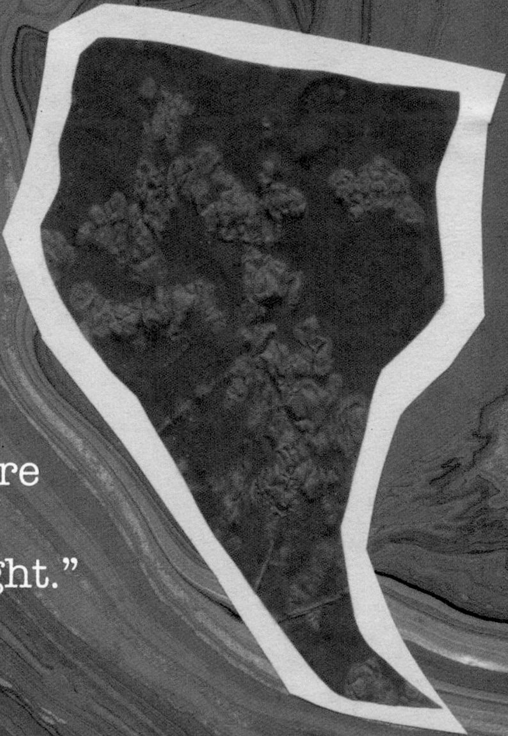

"Let there

be light."

And there was light.

It took Him just six days and six nights to finish

the continents and the oceans,

the moon and the stars,

and everything that swims, flies,

crawls, creeps,

and walks on two feet.

But it was a long six days.

On the seventh day, He decided to rest.

God also created a paradise,

a garden at a place called Eden.

And God let the first man

and the first woman

live in it.

Life was so perfect

and free of any troubles,

they hardly knew what to do with themselves.

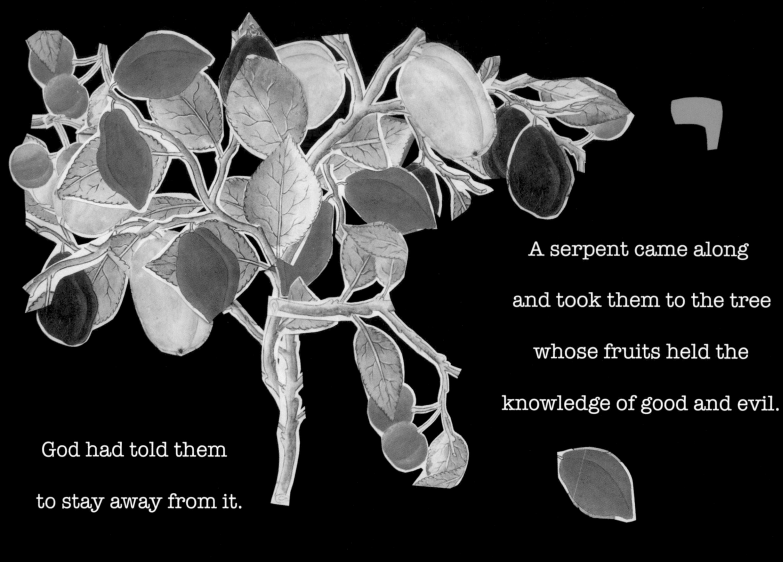

A serpent came along
and took them to the tree
whose fruits held the
knowledge of good and evil.

God had told them

to stay away from it.

But Adam and Eve ignored what God said.

They bit into the forbidden fruit
and found out more than humans were
perhaps meant to know.

So God made them leave

the garden

forever.

Adam and Eve's son, Cain, behaved even worse than his parents.

He killed his brother Abel because he was jealous of him!

God was very upset. He knew matters could not carry on like this much longer.

But on they went.

Adam and Eve's next son Seth lived until he was 912.

Seth's son Enosh made it to 905.

But it was Seth's great-great-great-great-grandson Methuselah

who survived the longest of them all, reaching the ripe old age of 969.

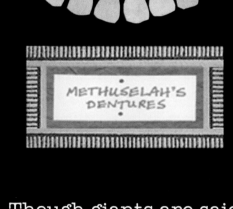

Though giants are said

to have roamed the earth then,

people still thought of men as the

most powerful beings God ever made.

Cleaning up creation

Methuselah's grandson Noah was the only person

who seemed to know right from wrong.

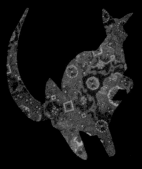

So God sent a flood

and told Noah

to save his family ...

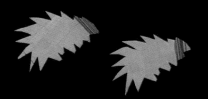

and two of every animal

on a very large ark.

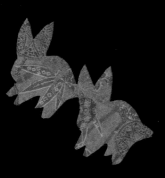

The rain lasted forty days.

The flood remained

on the earth

for another

one hundred and ten.

Hoping to find signs of dry ground, Noah sent a dove from the ark.

It returned with the fresh budding leaves of a young olive tree.

Once the waters had receded, God set a rainbow in the clouds

and promised never to send a flood that big again.

But the generations that followed Noah forgot about

how God had saved their ancestors.

Everyone spoke the same simple language then

and acted as if there was an answer for everything.

The sons of men even thought they were

as great as the Lord Most High.

To prove this to themselves, they tried

to build a city with a tower

that would reach the heavens.

This was a little too close

for God's comfort.

So He scattered them over the

face of the earth and created

the different languages

to confuse them.

From then on,

the place was called Babel,

because God had confused them.   God had turned their talk into babble.

First families

Abraham and his wife Sarah traveled many miles.

Leaving their hometown in ancient Iraq,

they went to live far up in the north for several years.

Then they headed south

for some adventures in Egypt.

Finally they settled in the land

that was then called Canaan.

Here God made a covenant with Abraham.

He promised that Abraham and Sarah would have

as many descendants as there are stars in the sky ...

and that Canaan would be their home.

Abraham did not have to sacrifice his son Isaac,

like many gods demanded their people do.

He did of course

have to prove that he was

ready to give God just as much.

So Abraham took Isaac

up Mount Moriah and prepared

an altar on which to surrender him.

At the last second,

God commanded him to hold back his knife!

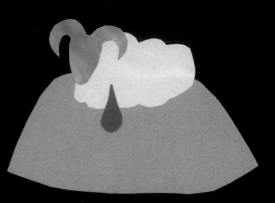

And that day,

Abraham sacrificed a ram

that God had sent instead.

God was keeping His promise about Abraham having descendants.

And Isaac grew up.

Isaac and his wife Rebecca had twins—

Esau, the hairy one,

who liked the outdoors ...

and Jacob, the smooth-skinned one,

who preferred reading and

helping his mother

to sporting and hunting.

Jacob, who had come out second,

was smarter and craftier than Esau.

When Isaac grew old and went blind,

Jacob pretended to be Esau and

won their father's blessing,

the birthright of the firstborn son.

As a grown man, Jacob even wrestled with an angel,

this time winning the Lord's special blessing.

God called Jacob "Israel" from then on, to mark the occasion.

Jacob married two sisters,

Leah and Rachel—

one plain and one pretty.

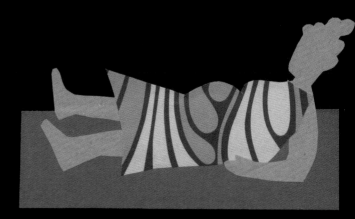

Between them (and their maids)

they had twelve sons.

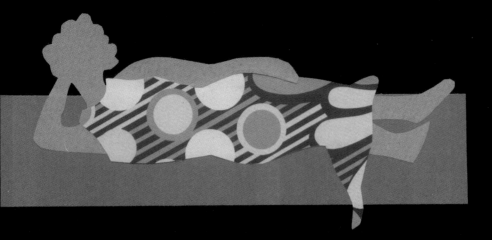

Naturally some tensions arose in the household.

Jacob made his

favorite son Joseph

an incredibly stylish coat.

Wearing it, Joseph told his brothers

how he dreamed they had

all bowed before him as a nobleman.

Joseph's brothers could not believe his nerve.

Furious that

he could

do no wrong

in their father's eyes,

the brothers sold

Joseph into slavery.

They told their father

that his dear boy had been eaten

by a ravenous beast.

Jacob felt like dying himself.

In Egypt Joseph's dreams came true as his wisdom led him
from prison rags to the princely life.

When famine hit the

land of Canaan,

the brothers went down to

Egypt in search of food.

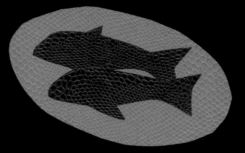

Fortunately Joseph had advised his

friend, the Pharaoh, to save plenty of it.

Bowing and begging before a man

they were told could help them,

Jacob's sons had no idea

this was their long-lost brother.

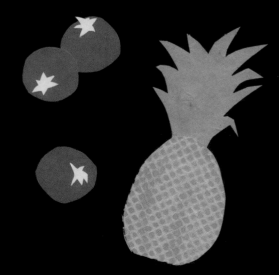

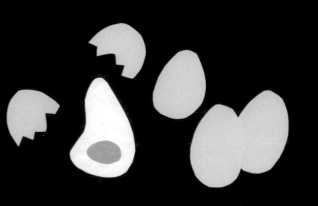

Joseph finally told them who he was
and saved his father Israel's

family from starving.

19

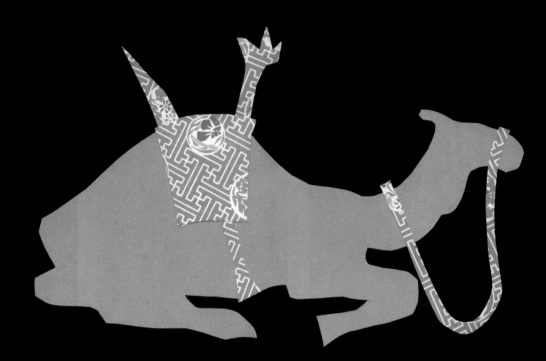

And Jacob got to see his

son once again.

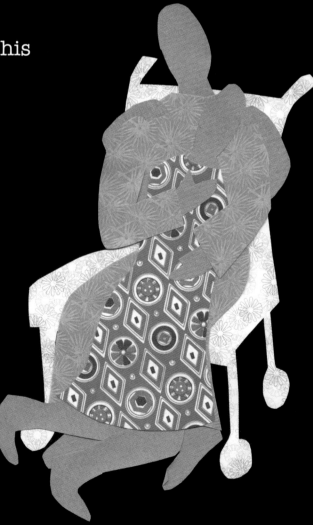

But the descendants of Israel did not all live happily ever after.

The Egyptians forced the Hebrews to be their slaves.

They made them gather stubble

for the straw they used

to make bricks

for the pyramids.

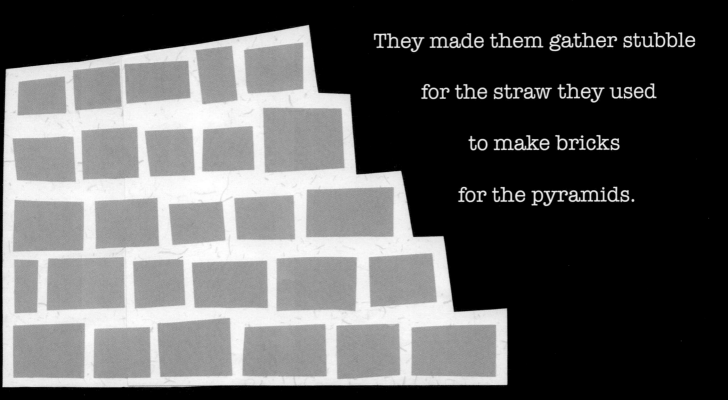

For many generations, the Hebrews worked impossible hours

gleaning away in the sweltering heat

without proper rest or pay.

He thought the slaves would

rise up and rebel against him.

So he ordered his men to kill

every son born to a Hebrew woman.

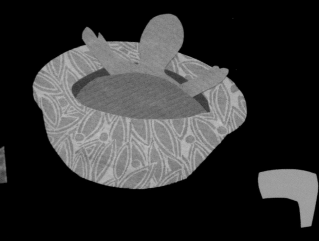

Wanting to save

her newborn boy from Pharaoh's wrath,

one mother sent

the unnamed child down the River Nile

in a basket

she had made herself.

An Egyptian princess found him,

drew him out of the water,

and called him Moses.

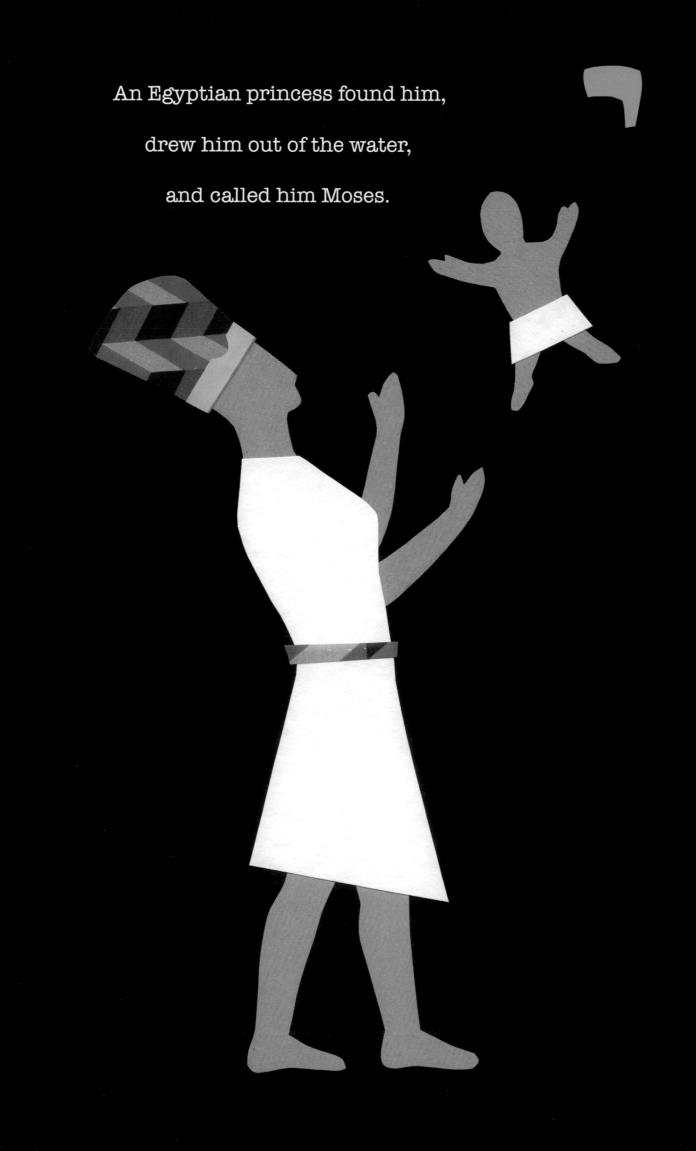

One day when he had grown up,

Moses saw an Egyptian hurting a Hebrew slave.

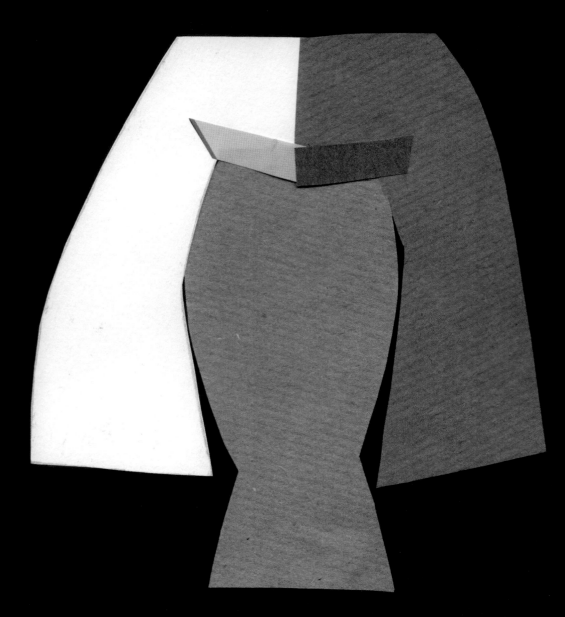

Moses was so furious

he killed the Egyptian and hid him in the sand!

Fleeing Pharaoh's police and escaping to the wilderness,

Moses suddenly met God in the form of a burning bush.

Moses was very afraid at first,

especially when he heard what God wanted him to do:

"I will send you to Pharaoh

so that you may bring forth

my people

the children of Israel

out of the land of Egypt."

Moses knew that Pharaoh would on no account let the people go ...

and that he would probably have Moses

thrown into prison for the rest of his life.

But after some persuasion, he agreed to go back.

God had chosen him to lead the people out of Egypt,

and His decision was final.

God proved He had the power to help Moses free the people

by punishing the Egyptians

with ten plagues.

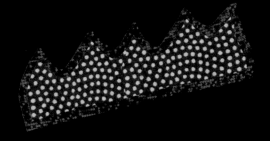

First He turned the Nile into blood.

Then He sent frogs,

and gnats,

and flies.

He killed the animals

that the Egyptians had kept

as food for themselves.

He caused sores to grow on every Egyptian,

spoiling even the Pharaoh's smooth skin.

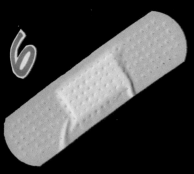

He sent hail to fire down

from the sky.

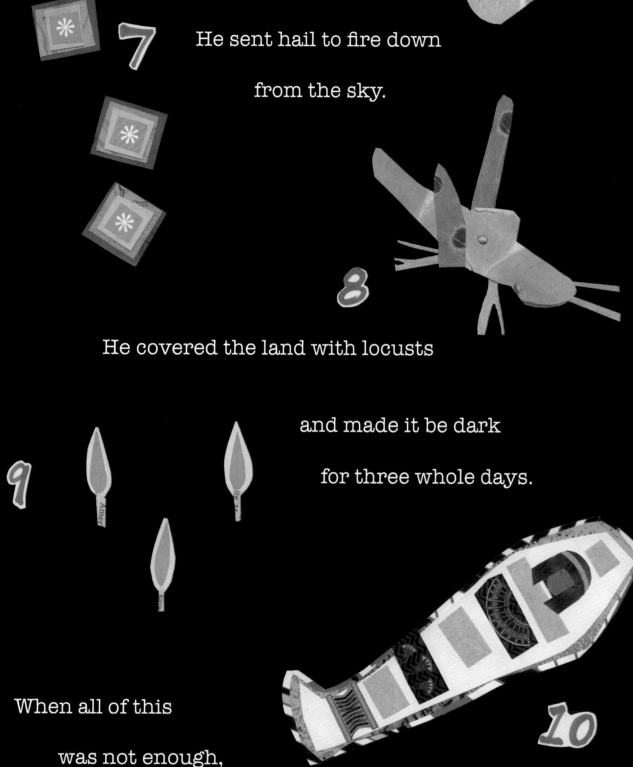

He covered the land with locusts

and made it be dark

for three whole days.

When all of this

was not enough,

He brought death upon the firstborn sons of Egypt

until Pharaoh finally let the people go.

Then God parted

the waters of the Red Sea,

so that all of the Hebrews

could escape safely to the other side.

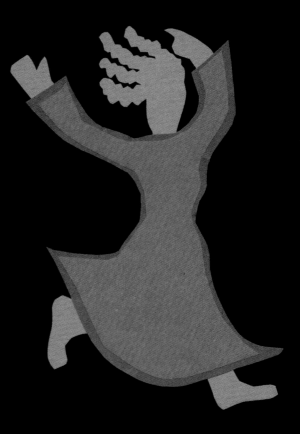

This historic liberation from slavery

is known as the Exodus.

The Lord had triumphed

gloriously over the Egyptians

who had pursued them.

Moses' sister Miriam led the song and dance

to celebrate the victorious flight from bondage into freedom.

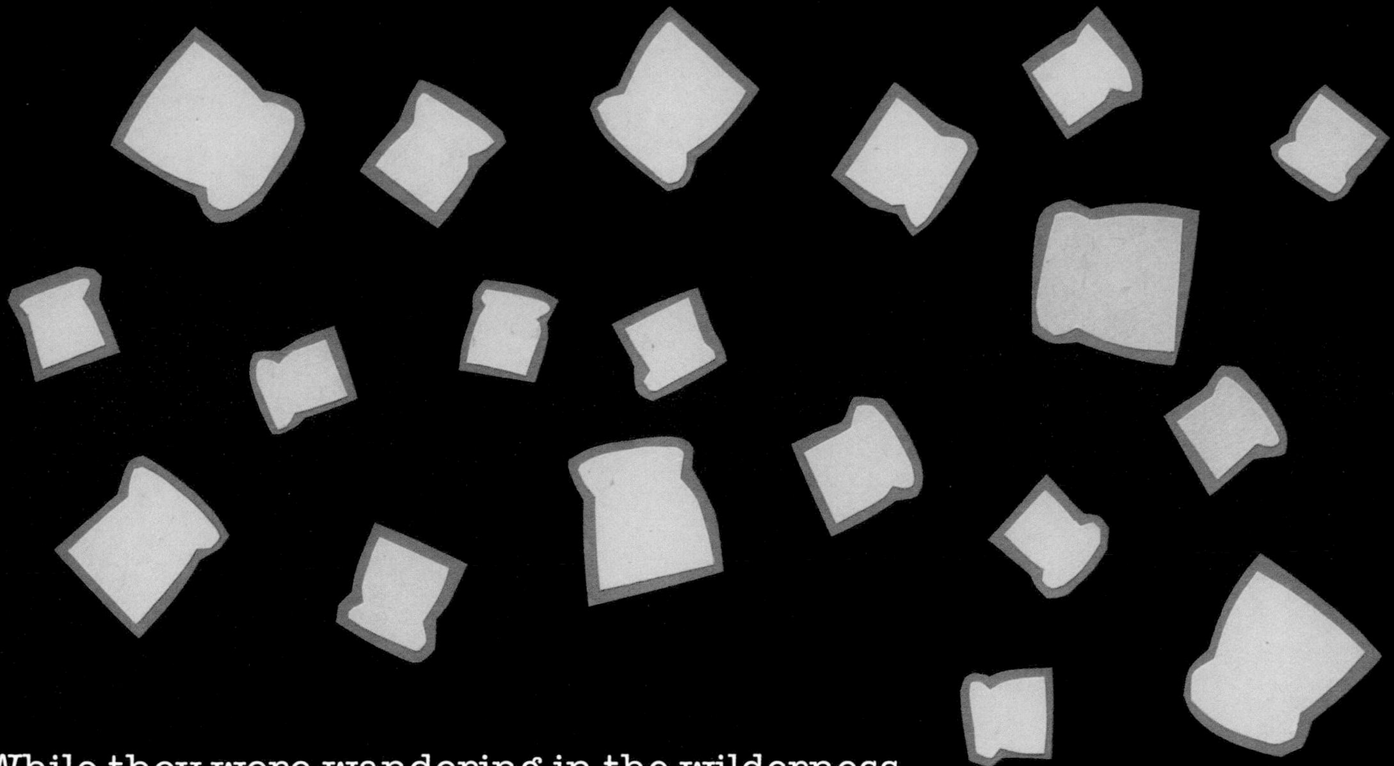

While they were wandering in the wilderness,

God saw that the people

were hungry and thirsty.

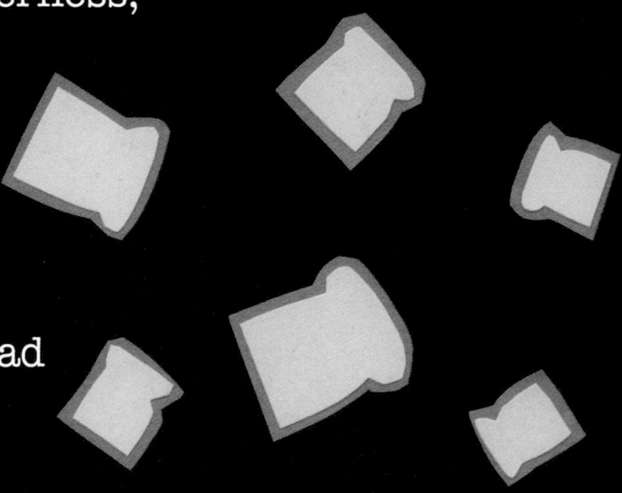

So He made deliciously flavored bread

rain down from the sky

and made water

flow forth from rocks.

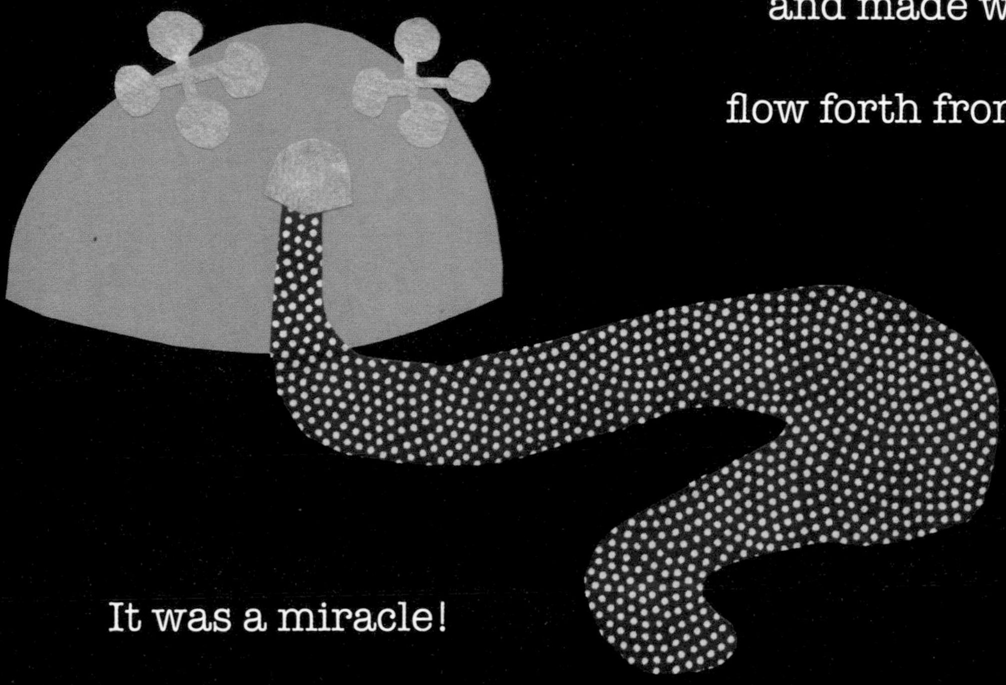

It was a miracle!

The deal was...

God then met Moses on Mount Sinai and made a covenant

between Himself and the people of Israel.

Spelling out the terms of the contract on two stone tablets,

God presented them with Ten Commandments.

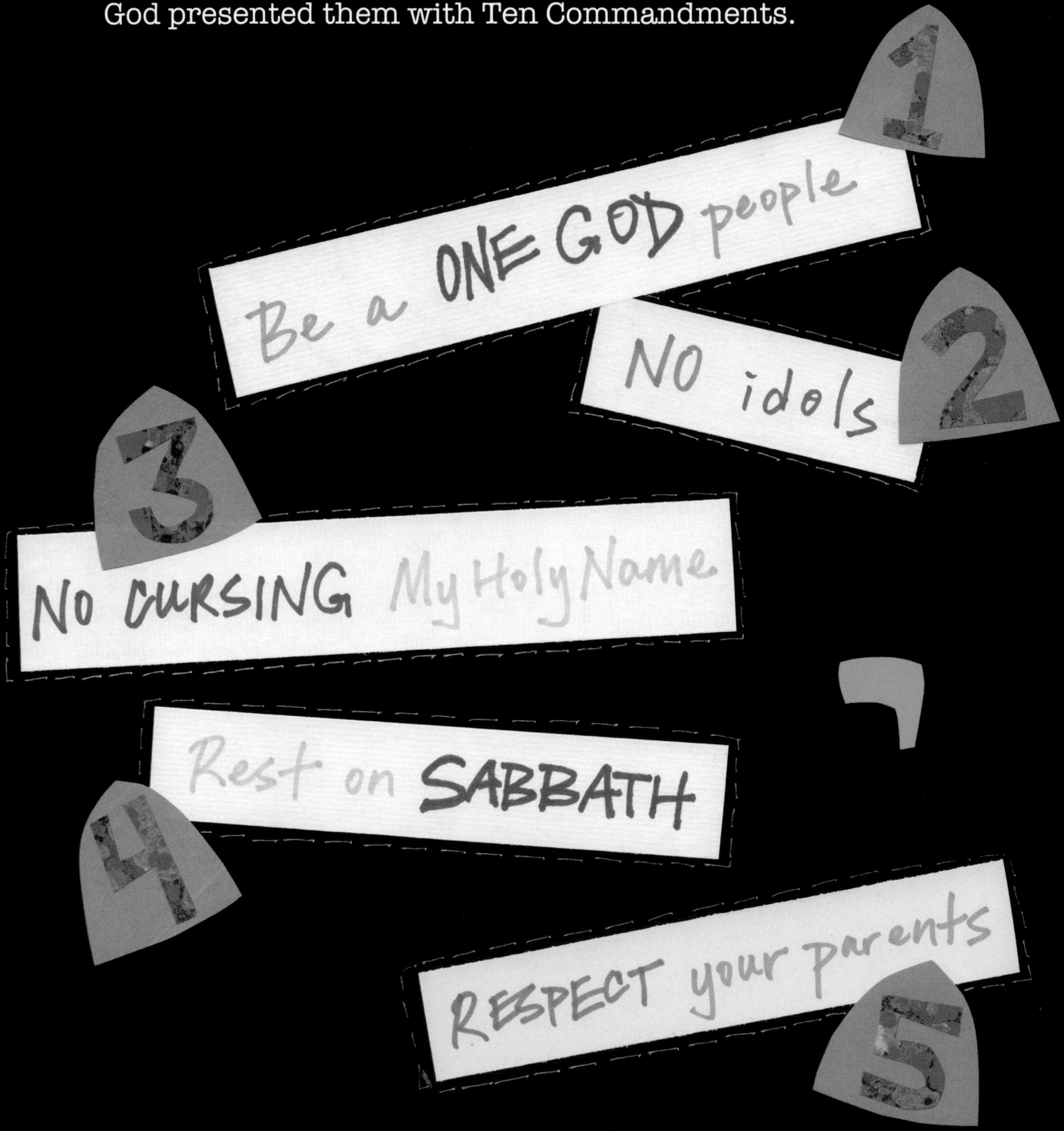

1 Be a ONE GOD people

2 NO idols

3 NO CURSING My Holy Name

4 Rest on SABBATH

5 RESPECT your parents

NO KILLING anyone 6

BE FAITHFUL to the one you love 7

The people agreed to all of God's conditions.

8 NO stealing

9 NO lying

NO jealousy 10

They promised to abide

by the holy laws,

to be faithful to God alone,

and to live in peace

with one another.

And God promised

to look after them

and one day give them rest.

The deal was done.

the people grew grumpy

and started to worship

a golden calf they had made.

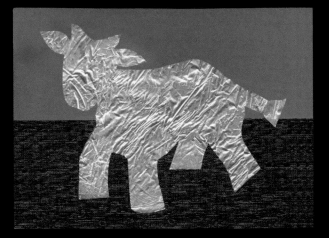

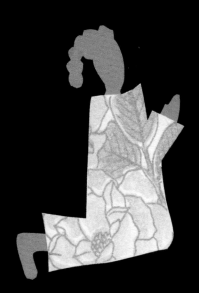

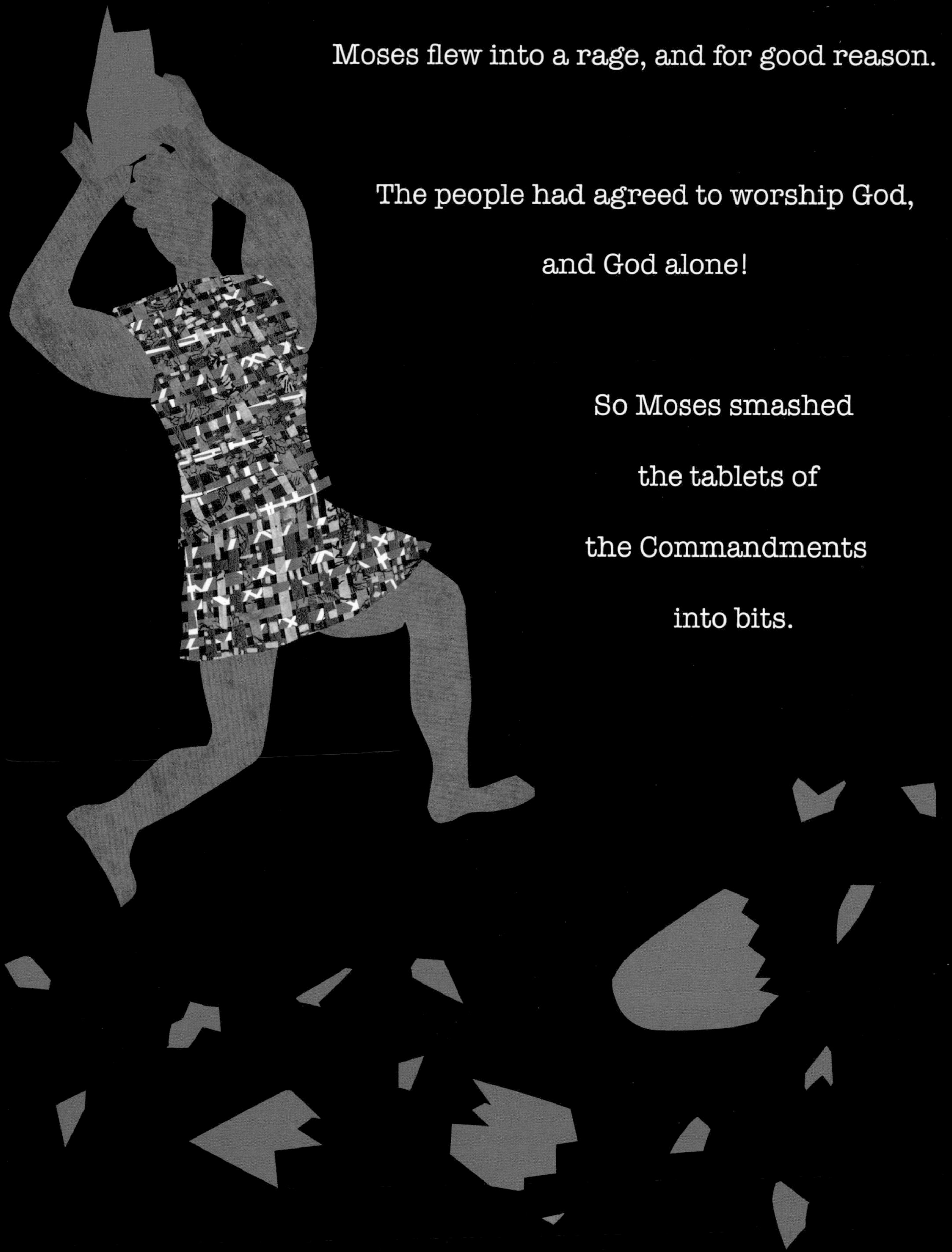

Moses flew into a rage, and for good reason.

The people had agreed to worship God,

and God alone!

So Moses smashed

the tablets of

the Commandments

into bits.

But God gave the people a second chance

and continued to lead them on their journey home.

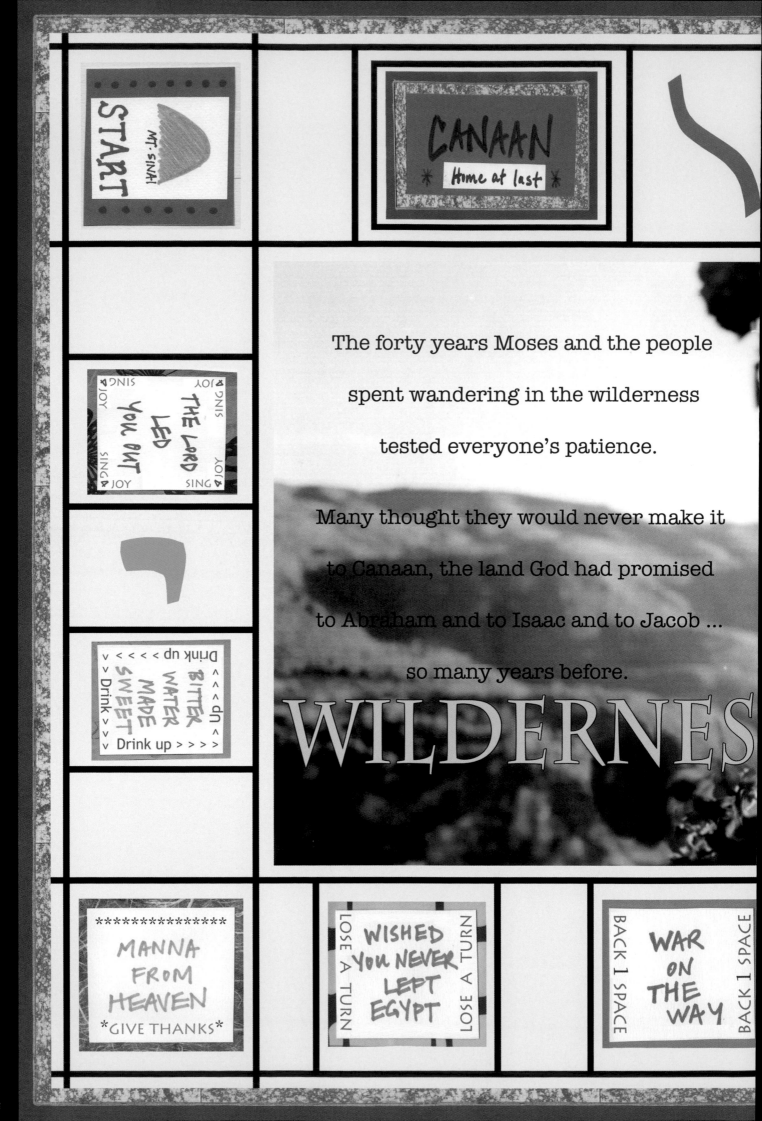

START
MT. SINAI

CANAAN
* Home at last *

SING JOY JOY SING
THE LORD
LED
YOU OUT
SING JOY JOY SING

BITTER
WATER
MADE
SWEET
Drink up > > >
< < < up < <
Drink > >

The forty years Moses and the people

spent wandering in the wilderness

tested everyone's patience.

Many thought they would never make it

to Canaan, the land God had promised

to Abraham and to Isaac and to Jacob ...

so many years before.

WILDERNES

****
MANNA
FROM
HEAVEN
GIVE THANKS

LOSE A TURN
WISHED
YOU NEVER
LEFT
EGYPT
LOSE A TURN

BACK 1 SPACE
WAR
ON
THE
WAY
BACK 1 SPACE

CROSS RIVER JORDAN · NEXT TURN ·

DEATH of MOSES
Moment of Silence

:: GO BACK TO START ::
CAUGHT WITH AN IDOL
:: GO BACK TO START ::

REMEMBER IN FUTURE
40 YEARS OF WANDERING ALMOST OVER
REMEMBER IN FUTURE

But the trek

continued.

3 spaces back
FORGOT ABOUT RED SEA
back 3 spaces

QUEST

a game for all ages

SABBATH SPACE
Rest and Roll

ROAD BLOCKED AT EDOM
» LOSE A TURN «

JORDAN

Throughout their travels,

the Israelites kept a shrine

to the Lord's presence

in a beautiful tent

called the tabernacle.

Aaron the brother of Moses was made a priest there

and placed in charge of the sacrifices.

He and his sons helped uphold

the numerous laws

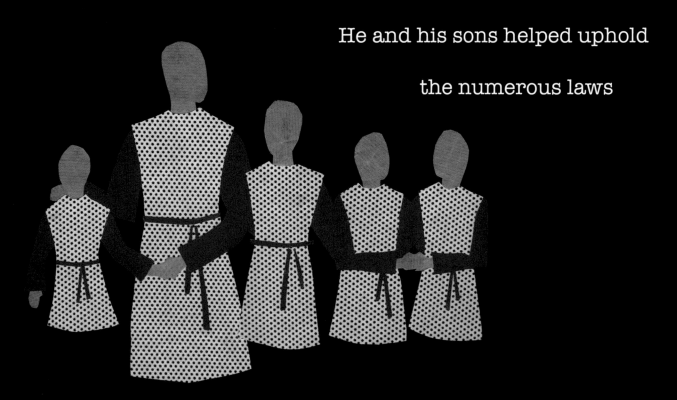

that God had added to the Ten Commandments.

Finally they crossed the River Jordan into Canaan,

and Joshua became

the leader of the people.

At Joshua's command

and with the sounding of many horns,

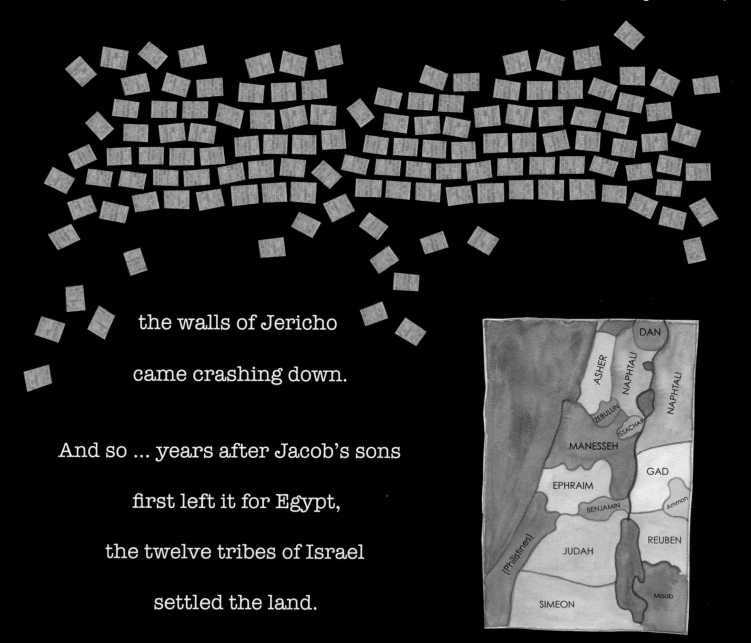

the walls of Jericho

came crashing down.

And so ... years after Jacob's sons

first left it for Egypt,

the twelve tribes of Israel

settled the land.

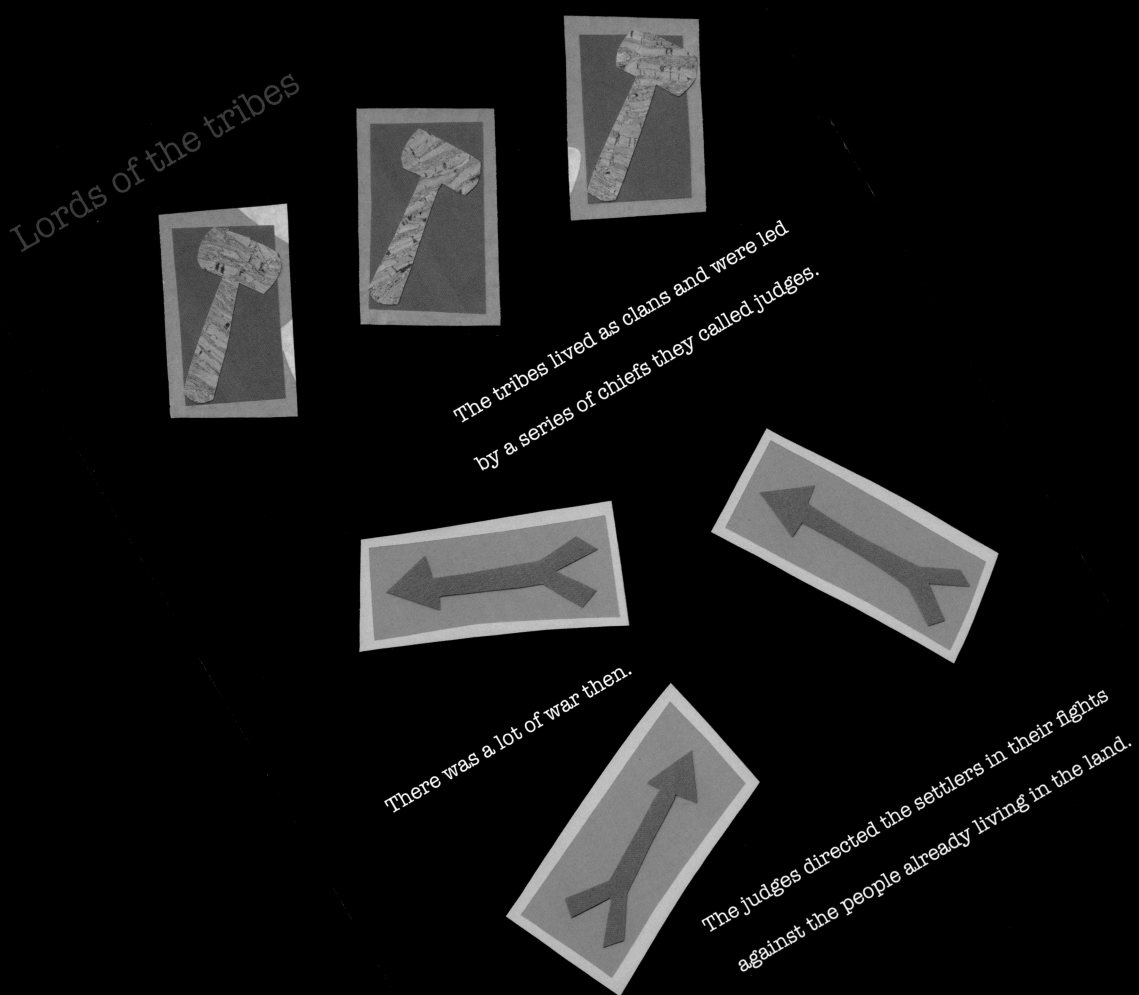

Lords of the tribes

The tribes lived as clans and were led by a series of chiefs they called judges.

There was a lot of war then.

The judges directed the settlers in their fights against the people already living in the land.

Deborah was both a judge and a prophet.

She gave army commanders

their battle orders.

She also offered her expert advice

to all who visited her

under her palm tree

in the hills.

The angel of the Lord

appeared before a

young judge named Gideon,

a man of valor.

The angel told him he would

lead the tribes of Israel to defeat their rivals, the Midianites.

Gideon conducted a "fleece-trial" just to be sure

that God meant what the angel said.

He left a piece of wool outside overnight,

hoping for God's sign in it by morning.

Though the ground was

covered in dew when he awoke,

the wool was completely dry.

He knew he and his army would win their next battle.

And so they did.

Samson was stronger than any man around.

He ate only healthy foods,

he drank no wine,

and he *never* cut

his divine hair.

He did not know his lover Delilah was

spying on him for the Philistines.

She discovered the secret to his power.

While he was sleeping,

Delilah instructed a servant to shave off

all seven of Samson's ever so long locks.

And Samson woke up weak.

But as his hair grew back,

so did his

strength

return.

He pushed over the pillars of the Philistine temple with nothing

but his bare hands!   It was a fitting finale.

During this era famine struck the land,

so Naomi and her family fled to Moab.

Here her husband died,

and her sons married foreign women.

When her sons also died and she returned

to Bethlehem, her daughter-in-law Ruth

insisted on going with her.

Though they were poor, they had each other.

In Bethlehem Ruth worked in the fields and

caught the eye of the landowner Boaz.

Within no time they married,

and they took

great care of Naomi.

Naomi had lost her husband and her sons,

but through Ruth's love she found

the comfort and company of family.

God would one day choose

Ruth's great-grandson David

to rule not just over a tribe, but over the whole of Israel.

42

A generation before David was born, a woman named Hannah

poured her heart out to the Lord.

God answered her prayer and gave her a son, Samuel.

Hannah dedicated his life to the Lord.

Samuel grew up to be an important judge and prophet.

One day when Samuel was counseling the tribes,

they asked if God could anoint a king for them.

Everyone wanted a single leader

so that they could be like the rest of the nations.

Samuel was not sure this was

such a good idea.

But God gave the people what they asked for.

The kingdom of Israel

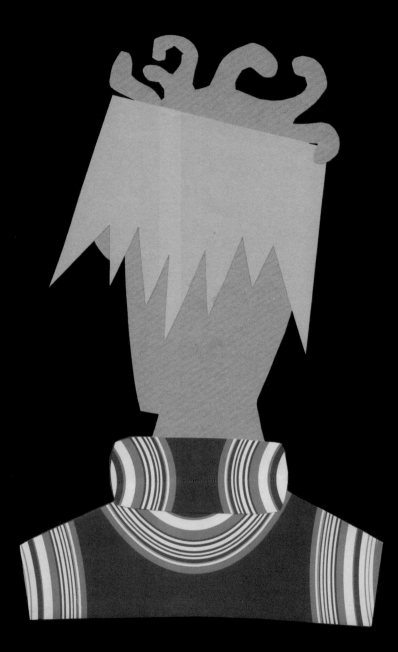

God first chose Saul, who went a little crazy as king.

Saul hired a dashing young shepherd from Bethlehem

to be his court musician.

This shepherd's name was David.

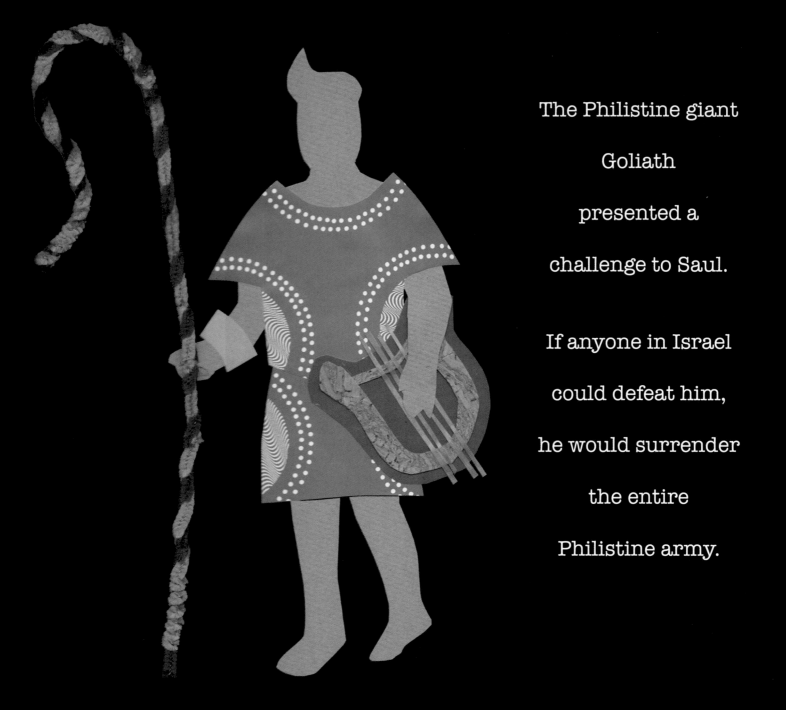

The Philistine giant

Goliath

presented a

challenge to Saul.

If anyone in Israel

could defeat him,

he would surrender

the entire

Philistine army.

Much to everyone's surprise,
David volunteered to fight the bully.

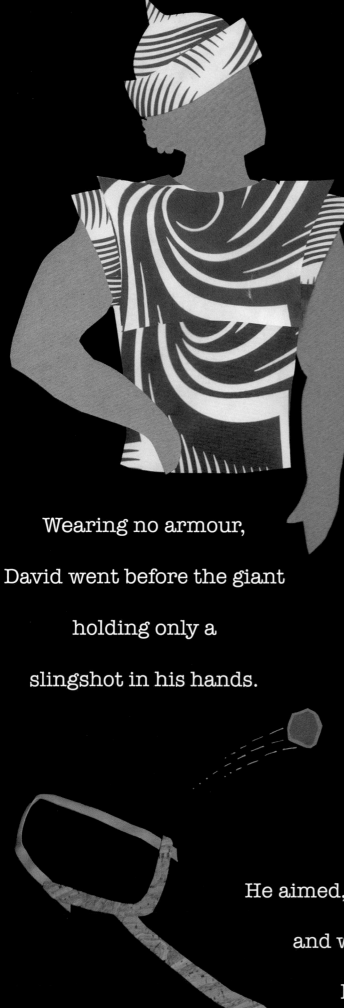

Goliath boasted that nobody

stood a chance against him,

especially not some

puny little pretty boy

from Bethlehem.

Little did he know,

David had something up

his sleeve.

Wearing no armour,

David went before the giant

holding only a

slingshot in his hands.

He aimed, fired,

and won,

killing Goliath in a single shot!

The ladies were

particularly impressed.

Then God made David king,

calling him His chosen one.

And David constructed

a fortress at Jerusalem

and made it the

capital of his kingdom.

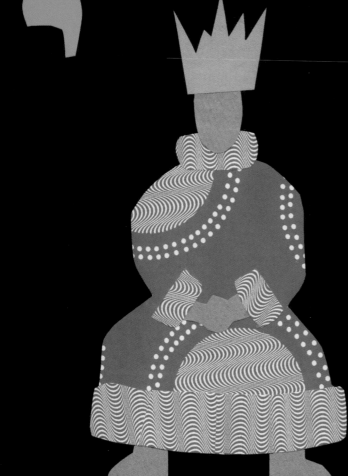

48

ZEBULUN BROS.
TEMPLE SAMPLES

David's son Solomon inherited the throne and built a majestic temple as a house for God in Jerusalem.

Divine home

Festival

Royal blues

Moses Morris

He was very wise,

very famous,

and had excellent taste.

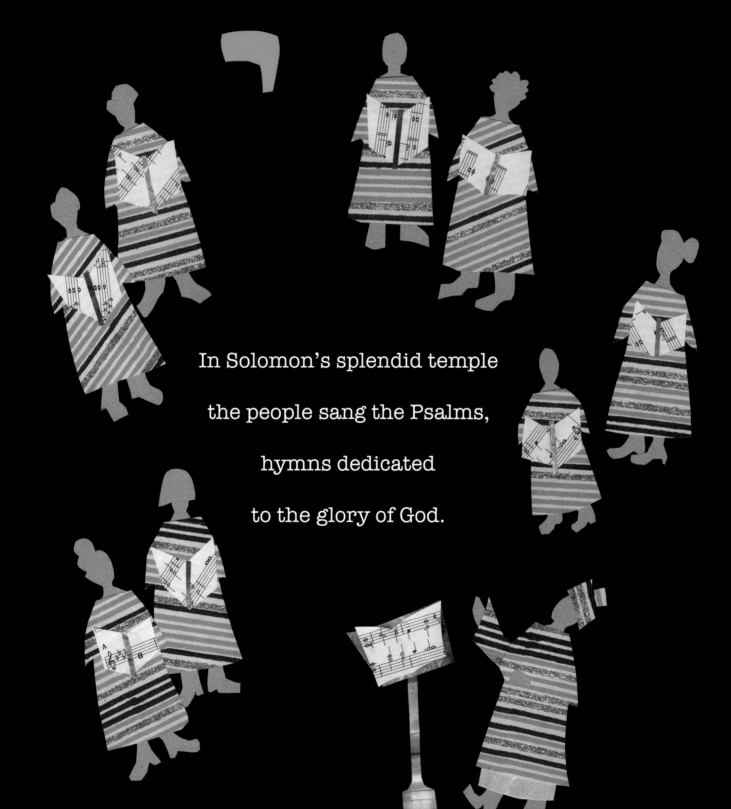

In Solomon's splendid temple

the people sang the Psalms,

hymns dedicated

to the glory of God.

There were also many well-read men in Solomon's court

who recited proverbs and

reflected on the ways of the world.

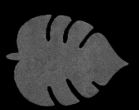

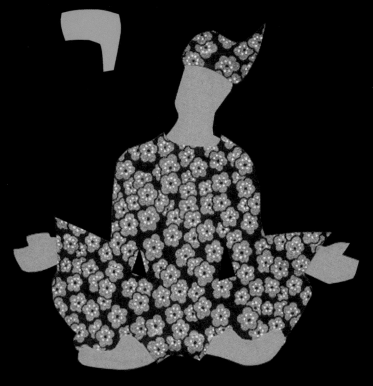

They knew that wisdom

was better than riches.

Life in Jerusalem had become very grand.

People came from far and wide to witness the spectacle of it.

Even the

Queen of Sheba

visited

Jerusalem.

She presented Solomon

with a generous selection of exotic gifts.

But she did not become one of his countless wives.

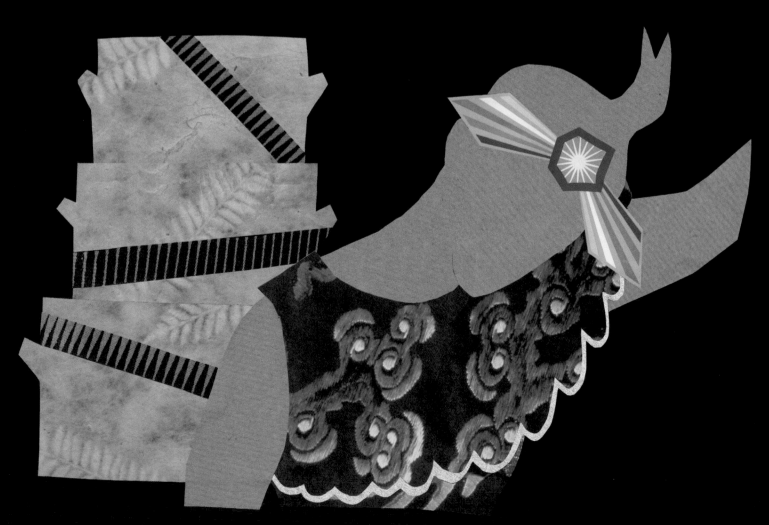

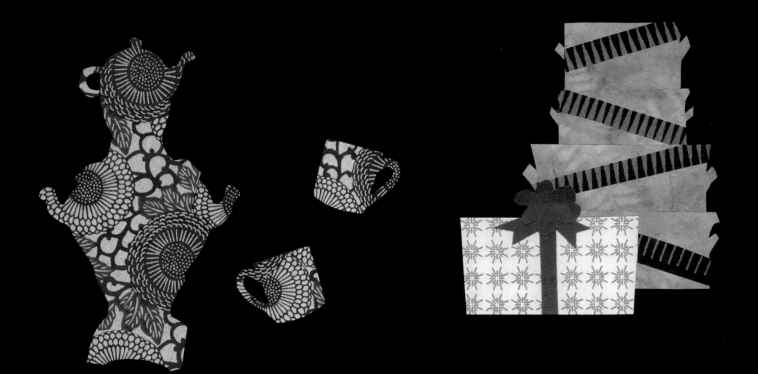

Solomon probably read her some of his poems.

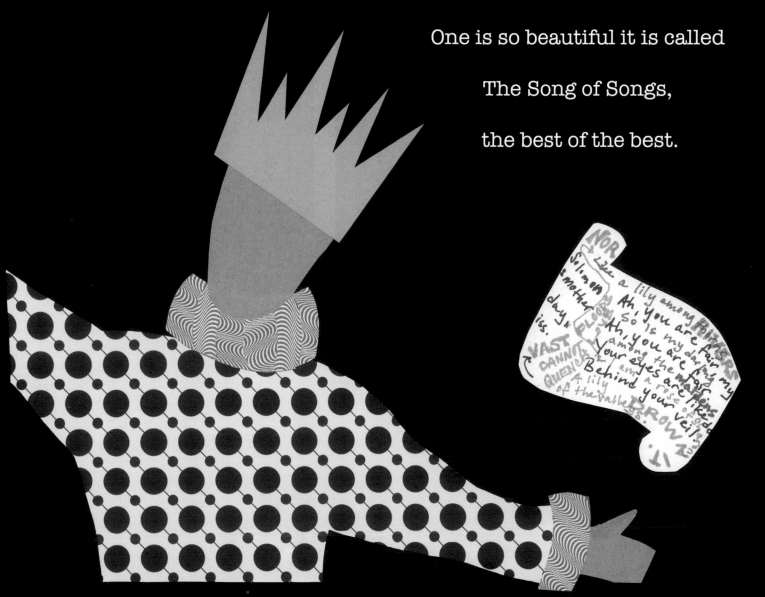

One is so beautiful it is called

The Song of Songs,

the best of the best.

When Solomon died,

the people in the north

decided they did not like his heirs.

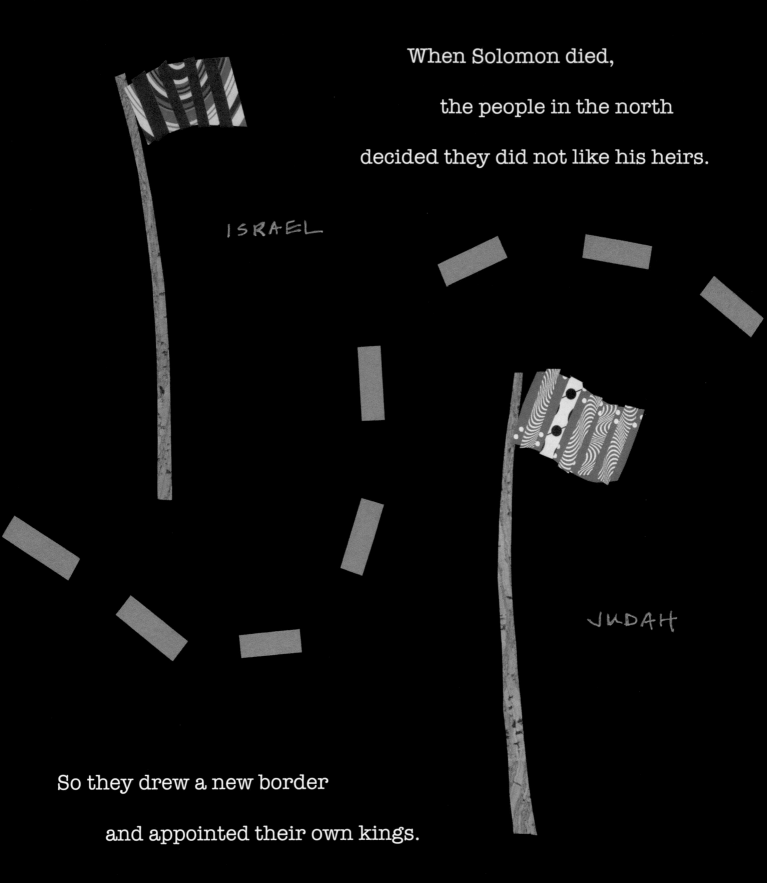

ISRAEL

JUDAH

So they drew a new border

and appointed their own kings.

The one kingdom was thus split into two:

Israel in the north and Judah in the south,

Prophets like Isaiah warned the new rulers

that if they did not work together

foreign nations could

easily invade them.

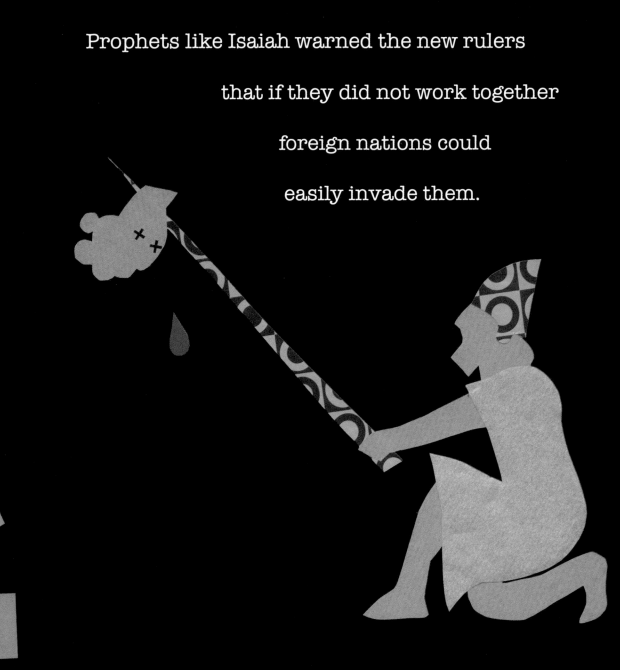

Ignoring the Commandments and neglecting the needy

would bring danger to Israel and Judah.

But the kings cared only about their own personal power,

when they were supposed to keep the people close to God.

The more the people of Israel and Judah forgot about
God's holy laws, the more selfish they became.

So some strange things started

happening to the prophets.

Elijah saw ravens bring him food

and angels make him cake.

He witnessed over fifty men

who worsipped foreign gods

burst into flames.

And at the end of his life,

he found himself

swept up to heaven

on a golden chariot.

Elisha discovered he could

purify water

as if by magic

and even bring a child

back to life.

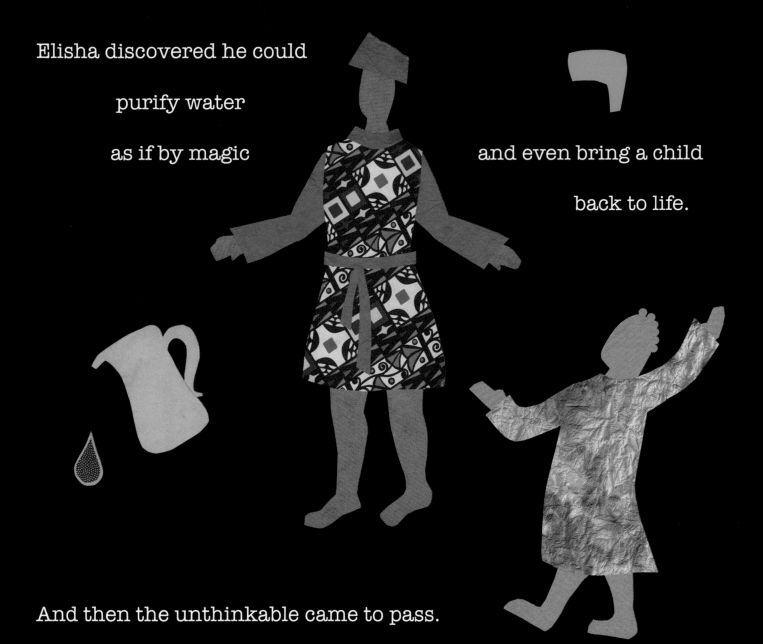

And then the unthinkable came to pass.

The Assyrians invaded the

northern kingdom of Israel,

so that only the southern

kingdom of Judah survived.

No one could believe the news.

When God ordered

the prophet Jonah

to tell the Assyrians

to repent and be saved,

Jonah tried to run away.

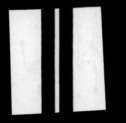

But he ended up being

thrown off a boat

and swallowed

by a giant fish ...

for three whole days.

The people of Judah and Jerusalem did not take the destruction of Israel properly to heart.

The rich got richer and laughed at the misery of others, while the priests made a mockery of sacrifice.

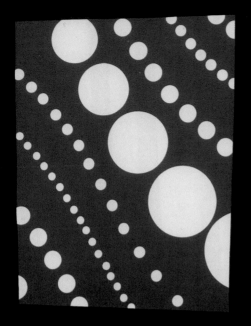

When Jeremiah was only a youth, God called him to be a prophet of the worst doom yet.

He told the people that they had one last chance to return to the ways of the Lord their God ... and that they were on a course to lose absolutely everything.

Judah and Jerusalem ignored everything Jeremiah was telling them.

Generation after generation failed to honor

their commitment to God.

But all of the prophets' predictions eventually came true.

God sent the Babylonians to conquer the land and to

take the king—and all the king's princes, prophets, and priests—

to be prisoners in Babylon.

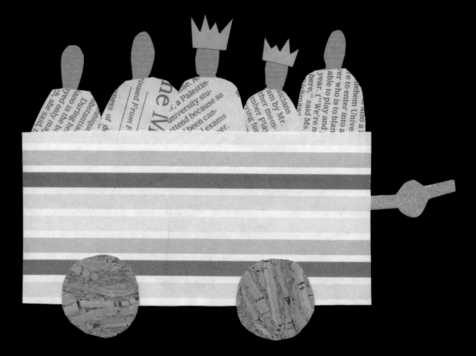

This was the beginning of a long time away from home

called the Exile.

Jerusalem meanwhile was an utter wasteland.

The Babylonians had toppled the temple and the city walls,

leaving only the poorest behind to clean up the rubble.

Then there was a man from the land of Uz, a foreigner named Job,

who lost his family and his fortune.

His friends were hardly a comfort.

They insisted his misery must have

been his own fault—

a punishment from God.

But Job had done nothing wrong.

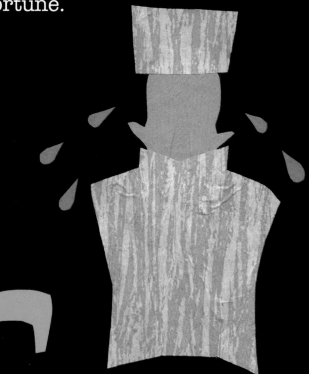

God finally spoke to

Job from a whirlwind,

showing him all the things in the

universe that had been too wonderful

for him to understand prior to this.

And Job took back some of the things he had

said in anger to his friends about God.

Then God restored Job with

twice as much as he had had before ...

which is a little bit like what happened to Israel next.

The empire period

Fifty years after the

fall of Jerusalem,

God sent Cyrus of Persia

to conquer the Babylonians.

Cyrus allowed

all the prisoners in

Babylon to return

to their homelands.

The Exile was over!

Cyrus even paid for the

temple and the walls of Jerusalem to be rebuilt.

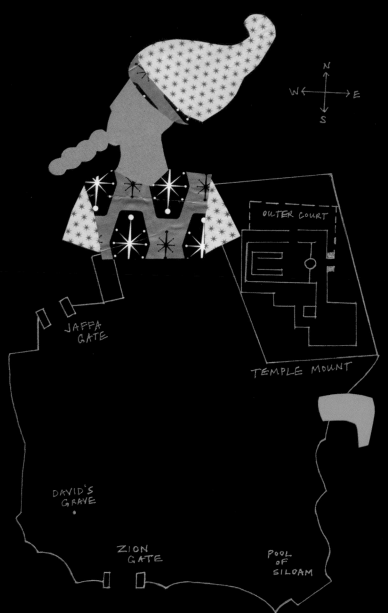

Ezra restored God's

law to the people,

and Nehemiah oversaw

the reconstruction.

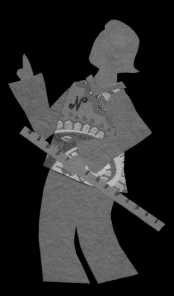

The Persian emperors granted the Jews

the freedom to live according to their own sacred laws.

One Jewish orphan named Esther

was exceptionally smart and breathtakingly beautiful.

She became queen

of the Persian Empire.

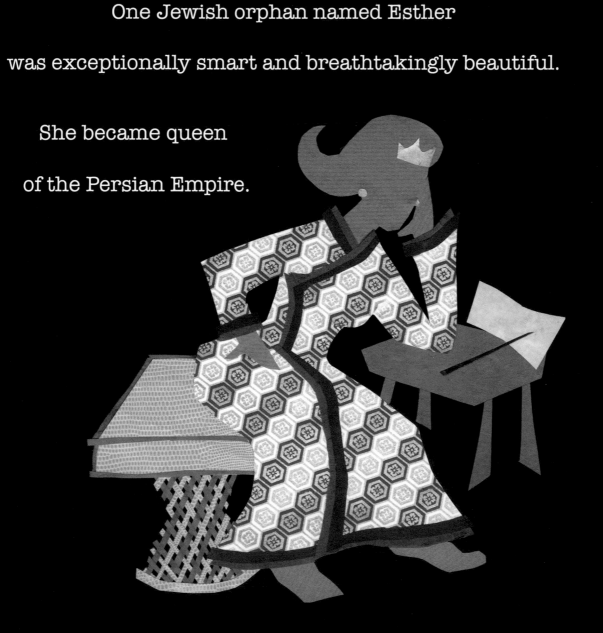

Esther used her power and her wits

to outsmart certain people who were jealous of the Jews.

She ensured that the law of the land

protected her people from harm.

Their civilization did not always practice compassion.

The Greeks demanded that

the people of Israel bow down to

their many gods ... or die!

Many Jews refused to betray

their one true God,

despite the threat of death.

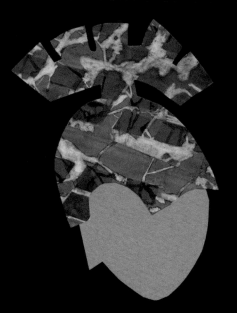

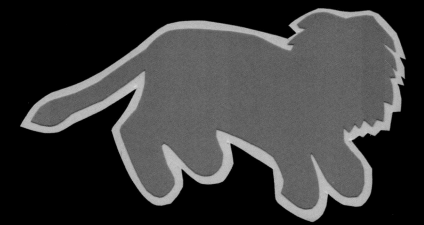

Daniel's faith was so strong,

he survived being thrown

into a fiery furnace.

Even the jaws of hungry lions

could not convert him, and he

passed through their den unscathed.

God was somehow there no matter how trying the times.

After all of these things came to pass,

the Romans took over the ancient world.

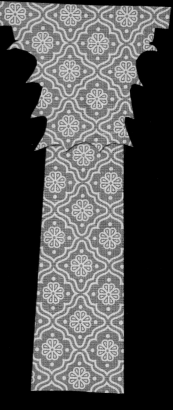

These rulers made the Jews pay enormous taxes

in order to fund the building of the empire's temples and coliseums.

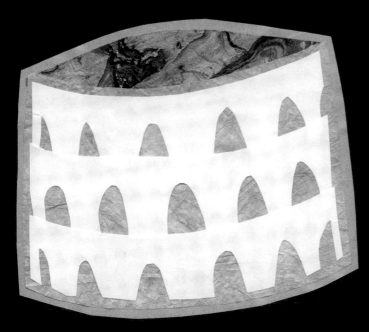

The Romans were so powerful,

it seemed too risky to revolt.

What happens next?

As the years rolled by the scribes of Israel decided

which books should be saved in their sacred library.

And they made copies of them

to preserve them for all time.

Some searched

the texts

for secret clues

about when

a new age of comfort

might come.

But the Romans did not like the fact that there was still

a temple to the Jewish God in Jerusalem.

When the Jews rebelled,

the Romans tore down all but

one wall of their temple

and sent them to live far away

from their promised land.

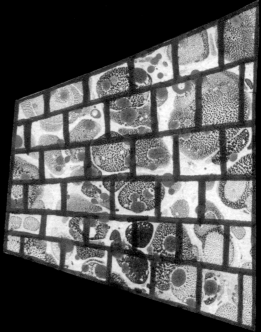

The rabbis read

the laws of Moses and

the other Scriptures

over and over

again.

They questioned

how life could go on

without a homeland.

But they found ways for people to abide by the holy laws

no matter where they lived.

And so God's faithful settled around the world.

By reading this story today, people of faith seek a relationship

with their one true God.

They look to it to keep the

Commandments, to seek justice,

and to love one another

as best they can.

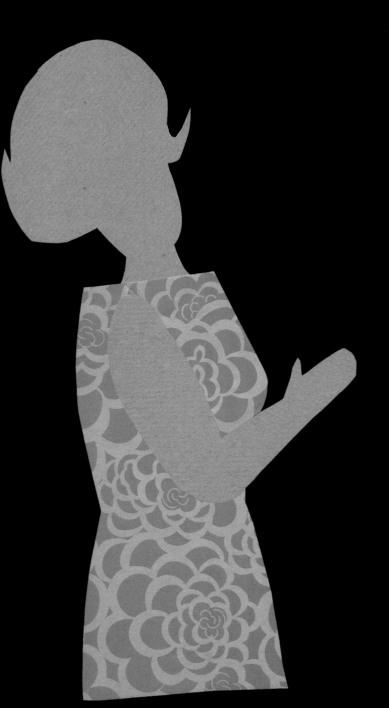

Remembering the promises

God made to Israel,

they believe the

future will be bright.

Though the Lord

sometimes works

in mysterious ways,

God continues to love us

and to guide

those who seek Him.

He still gives light and life

to the world and all of the

beautiful things in it.

Which means the story of

God and Israel ends

like a lot of good stories ...

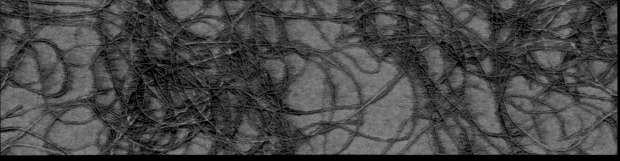

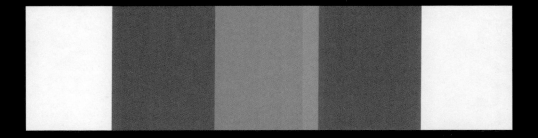

TO BE CONTINUED

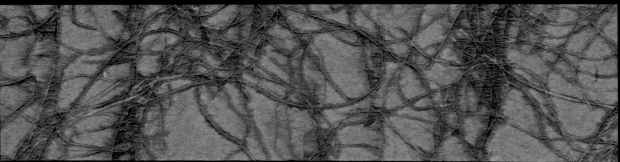

Read more

The Oldest Bedtime Story Ever

The Bible is indeed very old. Most of these stories were written down around 2,500 years ago. Many were memorized and passed down by word of mouth for hundreds of years before that.

The three faiths that share these stories all consider Abraham and Moses to be important ancient prophets. Moses was the first person to whom God revealed His name, when on Mount Horeb He said, "I am that I am."

Genesis, chapter 1, tells the story of the beginning from a cosmic perspective and ends with the Sabbath.

Genesis 2-3 explains how God created the first man from the ground and the first woman from his rib.

This story of Adam and Eve shows how human will disrupted the order of the world in the first chapter. For the earliest tale of sibling rivalry, in which God prefers Abel's sheep to Cain's grain, see Genesis 4.

The generations after Adam are listed in Genesis 5. Genesis 6:4 mentions mighty men, or giants, who roamed the earth before the Flood in Genesis 6-9.

The rainbow is the sign of the covenant God makes with all of humankind in Genesis 9. The sons of men build the Tower of Babel in Genesis 11.

God promises Abraham Canaan in Genesis 12. He only changes their names from Abram and Sarai to Abraham and Sarah in chapter 17. Isaac's trip up Mount Moriah and near-death experience are told in Genesis 22.

Esau and Jacob first clash in their mother's womb in Genesis 25. Two chapters later, Rebecca dresses Jacob up like Esau and helps trick her husband into bestowing his blessing on their second-born son. For Jacob's struggle with the angel, see Genesis 32. As a grown-up, Jacob faces family problems when he decides to get married. In chapter 29, he begins fourteen years working for Leah and Rachel's hands in marriage.

Joseph is introduced in Genesis 37 and in chapter 41 at the age of thirty becomes the Pharaoh's prime minister. The brothers first seek food in Egypt in Genesis 42.

The Pharaoh sends wagons to bring Joseph's family down to Egypt in Genesis 45. Jacob's emotional reunion with Joseph occurs in Genesis 46. Genesis ends with the burials of Jacob in Canaan and of Joseph in Egypt.

21   The Book of Exodus opens when the generations that followed Joseph and his brothers have multiplied. Fearing that the growing minority could turn against them, the Egyptians turn the Hebrews into slaves.

22-24   Moses is born into the house of Levi, put in the basket and found by Pharaoh's daughter in Exodus 2. The second half of this chapter shows him grown up and no longer able to live like a privileged Egyptian.

25   The Lord reveals Himself through the burning bush on Mount Horeb in chapter 3, but Moses refuses to go back to Egypt until the next chapter. It was not always easy for prophets to accept the missions God gave them.

26-27   The plagues begin in Exodus 7 and end with the Passover in chapter 12. God spares Goshen, where the Hebrews live, so that the torrents of pests, fire, hail, darkness, and death do not come to them.

28-29   Exodus 14 tells how Pharaoh changed his mind about letting the people go and sent his army after the people of Israel. Miriam's song of triumph (chapter 15) is one of the Bible's oldest poems. Manna, quails, and the greatest miracle in ancient plumbing follow in 16 and 17.

30-31   The Ten Commandments are dictated in Exodus 20 and repeated with minor variations in Deuteronomy 5.

32-33   Exodus 32 records how Moses' brother Aaron melted the people's gold earrings and turned them into an idol. In fury, Moses then breaks the tablets, burns the calf, and orders the people to consume the ashes.

34-35   The wilderness quest includes the laws and instructions given in Leviticus and Numbers. After convincing the stubborn people to agree to further conditions, Moses dies at the end of Deuteronomy. The Jordan dries up and the Israelites enter the promised land in Joshua 3.

36-37   Exodus 26-28 lays out the plans for the tabernacle and is the first time Aaron and his sons wear their holy garments. Their role as custodians of the law becomes official in Leviticus 8. Jericho falls in Joshua 6.

38-39   The Book of Judges describes the conflicts Israel faced with the people already living in the land. Deborah directs the defeat of the Canaanite army in chapter 4.

40-41   Gideon meets the angel in Judges 6 and subdues the Midianites in chapter 8. Samson is born at the end of Judges 13 and loses his hair three chapters later.

42-43   The Book of Ruth is just four chapters and has a happy ending. God answers Hannah's prayer in 1 Samuel 1 and calls the boy to be a prophet in chapter 3.

By asking for a human king, the people fail to see that God Himself is king. Samuel warns that kings will only tax them and turn them into slaves in 1 Samuel 8. 44

The most handsome man in all Israel (1 Samuel 9), Saul is anointed prince by Samuel and hailed king by the people in chapter 10. The chapters that follow show how he quickly loses their favor as well as his own sanity. 45

In 1 Samuel 16, God sends Samuel south to Bethlehem in Judah, where he anoints Jesse's youngest son with oil. The showdown with Goliath quickly follows in chapter 17. 46-47

After a tense twenty chapters, Saul falls on his own sword and David becomes king over Israel and Judah (2 Samuel 5). Solomon, son of David and Bathsheba, begins his reign in 1 Kings 1. Chapters 6-7 recount the seven years it took to build the temple, compared to the thirteen years Solomon devoted to the royal palace. 48-49

The Book of Psalms is the ancient hymnal. Books such as Proverbs and Ecclesiastes contain the wisdom of the age. 50-51

The queen of Sheba arrives in 1 Kings 10. The Song of Songs is understood to be a special book of love poems. 52-53

The prophets knew that life under kings would only go from bad to worse. The country splits in 1 Kings 12. 54-55

Elijah and Elisha are just two of the many prophets to encounter God's odd demands and powers. Elijah's adventures begin in 1 Kings 17. He ascends to heaven in 2 Kings 2. Elisha's miracles immediately follow. Several generations later, in 721 BCE, Assyria brings the kingdom of Israel to an end (2 Kings 17). 56-57

Jonah is one of the shortest books in the Bible. Jeremiah is the longest. 58-59

The Book of Lamentations and the ends of 2 Kings and 2 Chronicles all describe the tragedy Jerusalem experienced at the hands of Babylon. The Exile started with deportations in 592 and 587 BCE and lasted over fifty years. Many consider the Book of Job to be an allegory of Israel's experience in exile. 60-61

Cyrus declares that the exiles can go back in the Book of Ezra. In the Book of Nehemiah the city walls are rebuilt. 62

In the Book of Esther a young woman saves her people by capturing the king of Persia's heart. 63

64-66   Though set in Babylon, the Book of Daniel was composed centuries later during the years of Greek persecution (c. 167-163 BCE). The beasts in the second half of the book secretly represent foreign rulers. The Hebrew Bible stops before the Romans come to power; but under their oppressive rule, Jewish leaders agreed which writings would be included in their canon.

67   The loss of the temple and life in diaspora compelled rabbis to write down their interpretations of Scripture. These are known as the Talmud and the Mishnah.

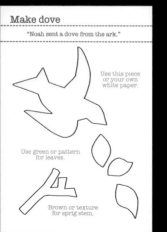

Make dove

"Noah sent a dove from the ark."

Use this piece or your own white paper.

Use green or pattern for leaves.

Brown or texture for sprig stem.

Make it yourself

To make your own versions of the illustrations in this book, visit www.biblebeautiful.com. This site includes tips and templates to help you create collages at home. Proven to bring light to any rainy day.

The fine print

The illustrator would like to thank everyone who gave permission to use their copyrighted material. Title page ribbon from Annabelle Lewis for VV Rouleaux.

pages 1-3

"A book about God" features stars by Mani-G'Raps and clippings from Günter Haseloff's 1938 study of medieval psalm illustrations. Menorah background © American Library Association (used with permission); fish, "Lord" and "El" paper from Hana Yuzen.

4-6

Marbled paper by Artoz and continents of green vellum from Kate's Paperie, New York. God sleeps under Mani-G stars.

7

Adam and Eve bask beside William Morris Willow Boughs (© V&A Images/ Victoria and Albert Museum) and spotted Yuzen origami paper.

8-9

Tree cut from Tradescant's Old English Orchard (© The Bodleian Library, University of Oxford); serpent mesmerizes in Matrix by Chione & Lorenz. Cain's Oh, Boy! stripes can't compete with Abel's Red Olives marbled paper from Paper Source.

10-11

Museum borders copied from A. Raguenet's Matériaux et Documents (c. 1905). Rabbits wait to board the ark in Hana Yuzen.

12-13

The Tower of Babel includes blocks of text cut from Japanese calligraphy, a Spanish architectural catalogue, Haseloff's German manuscript, biblical Hebrew flashcards by Visual Education, and a handwritten translation of the chapter in isiXhosa.

14-15

Abraham and Sarah make their pledge in South African shweshwe from Da Gama and in Design Design, Inc.'s Blum Casuals. Young Isaac's pattern is from Senegal.

16-17

Leah and Rachel recline in Heal & Son maternity wear (© V&A Images/Victoria and Albert Museum).

18-19

Brothers' hand-me-downs from Design Design, Inc. Joseph's couture coat crafted from Yuzen paper. Snakeskin paper for the fish he serves is from Soolip.

20-21

Traditional kimono prints on origami paper clothe Joseph and his camel on their emotional reunion with Jacob. Father Israel's geriatric garb from Sam Flax, New York. As a slave, the Hebrew woman wears no pattern and plucks stubble made from newsprint.

22-23

Moses drifts down the Nile in olive-oil packaging amidst bulrushes of "Fritillaria, Walberswick" (1915) by Charles Rennie Mackintosh (© Hunterian Museum and Art Gallery, University of Glasgow, Mackintosh Collection, 2012); Egyptian headdress from a 1930s Heal & Son pattern (V&A Images/Victoria and Albert Museum).

24-25

Bush of Kate's Paperie cork paper burns bright in gold marble from Artoz.

26-27   In the plagues, hailstone paper purchased at MXYPLYZK, New York; locust cut from a photograph by Joseph Scheer; mummy edged in a border from Heal & Son (© V&A Images/Victoria and Albert Museum).

28-31   Blue Red Sea paper from Hana Yuzen. Commandments numbered in Second marbled paper printed at Compton Marbling, Tisbury, UK.

32-33   Idol worship takes place in napkins from Norman and Krista Blake. Moses makes a bold statement in a bouclé hand-woven from four assorted papers.

34-35   Photograph of an Andalucian valley courtesy of Alex Tehrani, with game-space borders purchased at Kate's Paperie and Mélodies Graphiques, Paris. Egypt border © Bethge, Hamburg; Red Sea border by Katalin S. Perry.

36-37   A Yuzen valance frames the tabernacle's interior from Fortnum & Mason. Aaron and his sons are prim as priests in polka dots by Da Gama. Joshua wears herringbone tweed opposite a ram's horn patterned from Salvador Dalí's "Song of Songs of Solomon" series.

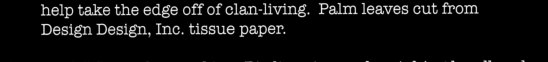

38-40   Deborah and the other judges find traditional tartans by Gordon Flavell help take the edge off of clan-living. Palm leaves cut from Design Design, Inc. tissue paper.

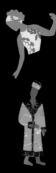

41   Delilah keeps her cool in a Birdtree top and matching headband by Neisha Crosland.

42-44   Boaz sets his eyes on Ruth in a Cardinal cloak from Snow & Graham trimmed in two-tone floral from Roger La Borde. Hannah puts her son on a pedestal in South African shweshwe from Da Gama. Protesters wear traditional kimono prints, opposite Samuel's Heal & Son sleeves (© V&A Images/ Victoria and Albert Museum).

45-47   For his portrait, Saul wears Small Ovals by Neisha Crosland. David's Watermark ensemble and Goliath's Spin armor are also by Neisha Crosland.

48-49   More royal couture from Neisha Crosland, with Solomon showing his style in a Beaded Stripe robe contrasted with his father's Watermark trim. Fortress assembled from a visitor's guide to Oriel College, Oxford. Temple swatches include Brookfield's Indigo Blossom and William Morris patterns (© V&A Images/Victoria and Albert Museum).

50-51   Victorian Psalms border developed from a pattern by Mintons; choir robes from Kate's Paperie. The wise man contemplates the seasons in Yuzen blossoms.

52-53   Sheba stays chic in a chinoiserie cape and gown (Dragon patterned silk tapestry, © Ashmolean Museum, Oxford), with accessories by Mani-G'Raps and Neisha Crosland. Ewers and samovar from Hana Yuzen; handled urn by Katalin S. Perry; hookah and traveling trunk papers purchased at Kate's Paperie; origami giftwrap from London Graphic Centre; packing tape from Da Gama.

54-55   Assyrian's helmet and spear by Line Creative, UK.

Elijah is ready for the ride of his life in a Windham Fabrics swatch sold at the   56-57
Harriet Beecher Stowe House. Elisha looks miraculous in a Viennese motif by
Josef Hoffman (© Pomegranate Communications, California).

Jonah's bubbles and stripes are from Heal & Son (© V&A Images/Victoria   58-59
and Albert Museum); fish skin from a photograph by Lucy Skaer ("Scorpion/
Diamond, Amsterdam", © 2001). Jeremiah labors on in patches of
reconfigured newsprint – his lament echoed in Neisha Crosland's Dotty paper.

Fallen royals are carted off to Babylon in prison stripes purchased at Kate's   60-61
Paperie. Job's mourning dress purchased at the Artstore, Glasgow;
whirlwind includes portions of a photograph of Jane Anderson Morse.

Cyrus shows off his star quality in a tunic purchased at MXYPLYZK and   62-63
sleeves and headgear by Design Design, Inc. Nehemiah's top purchased at
Papyrus, New York. Coiffed for court, Esther gives her people glamour
in a Yuzen cloak and upon a handwoven snakeskin stool.
Pashmina and silk carpet border from a 17th-century Mughal design
(© Ashmolean Museum, Oxford).

Greek helmet cut from a catalogue with Graham Dean's "Tuo Edisni/Inside   64-65
Out" (© Steven Lacey Gallery, London, 2001). Roman Corinthian column
paper purchased at Blick, New York.

The Western Wall of the temple stands tall in brown Rotring ink on Sylvie   66-67
Hournon's marbled paper. Rabbi and son talk text in sober threads from
Kate's Paperie.

This modern mother celebrates Sabbath in style, in a Rosa dress by Neisha   68-69
Crosland. Alexander "Greek" Thomson railings photographed by the author
in Glasgow's West End.

Blue floss paper from Kate's Paperie; stripes cut from a giftwrap by   70
Caroline Gardner, UK.

Every attempt was made to contact and credit sources.

The Oldest Bedtime Story Ever

is published as a narrated digital edition

and in hardback by

ORSON & CO

New York, NY.

www.orsonandco.com

The Bible Beautiful Series:
The Oldest Bedtime Story Ever

ISBN 978-0-9858135-0-5

8 7 6 5 4 3 2 1

This book was printed in America.

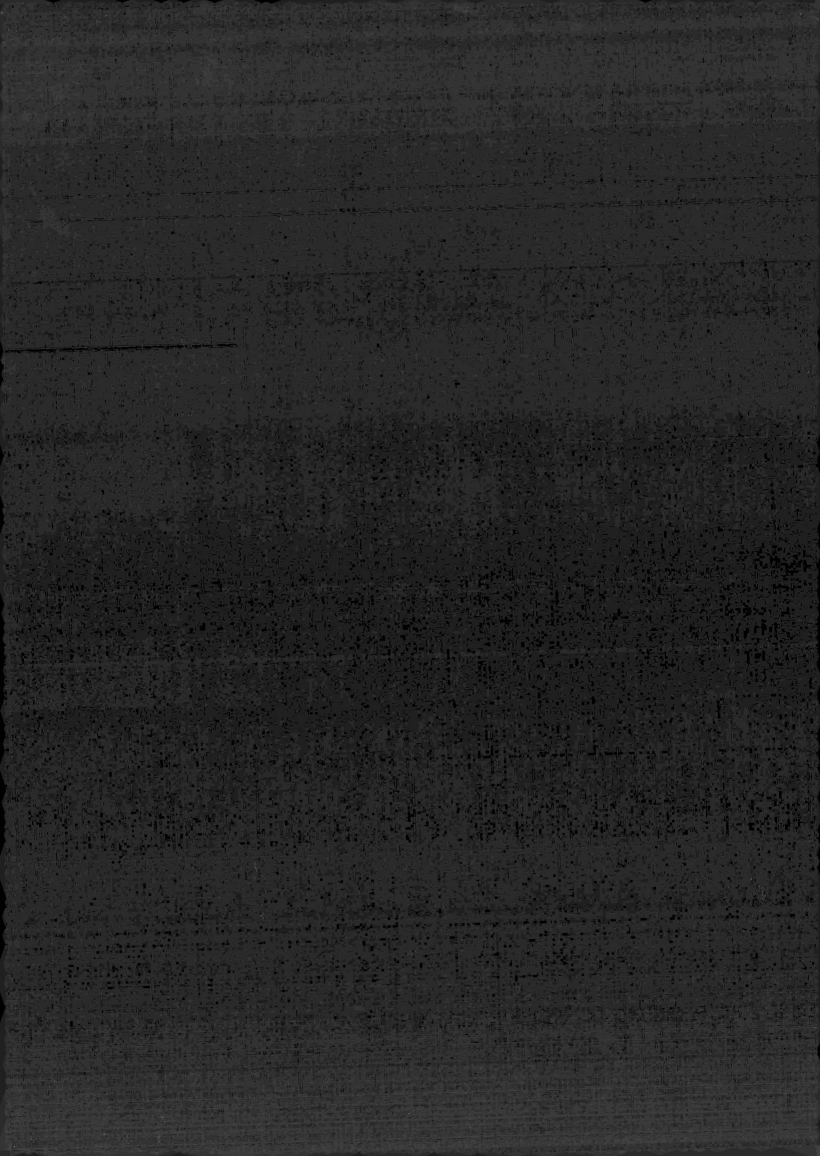